The Wealth of Wisdom

Sam Nnodim

This Book was printed in the United States of America.

ISBN: 9785033775

ISBN-13: 978-9785033779

Chiysonovelty International

chiyson@minister.com

To order additional copies of this book, contact:

Sam Nnodim

234-8037026735

www.samdimcomputers@yahoo.com

CONTENTS

"*Every reasonable man or woman will work hard to produce fruit that will feed generations even after he has gone.*" – Sam Nnodim

DEDICATION

I dedicate this book to God Almighty.

INTRODUCTION

LIFE is Learning, Intimacy, fame and Eternity! In life, there are those who have learnt the basic fundamental rules of the game of life through physical understanding and temperance. They have experienced the things of life and found out the truth for themselves. They have perfected their ability to make things happen, came out with their true mettle and assessed what they wanted to accomplish in their lives, their purpose.

These great beings have developed their self-confidence, faith and courage. They have truly experienced the living process and refused to get hooked on a feeling, sensation or addiction. Rather they used their addiction as a means to escape and develop habits that made them who they are.

They attained their greatest successes and experienced their greatest failures. They learnt how to reach down to the very core of their being and pulled out just a little bit more of whatever was needed. They created in themselves something that extends beyond the boundaries of their lifetime, having reached within and summoned the forces and vibrations that they can initiate and direct in the present.

In this day and age, these great beings are the living embodiment of our ongoing history. The wisdom of these elders is our most valuable resource.

And their insights can help us, especially our younger generations, determine where we are going. The wealth of Wisdom gives us the valuable abundance of the principal thing, and offers all of us a chance to cultivate those strong forces and vibrations to create a presence that will continue to grow beyond our lifetime.

I strongly believe that young people in particular, will understand learning, intimacy, fame and eternity better through the Wealth of Wisdom from our elders whose commitment and abilities shaped our community.

They impressed and inspired! And I have no doubt that after reading this masterpiece, you will be empowered to see things as they can be, rather than as they appear to be so that you too can address a positive, worthwhile need in our community and in the world.

The Life-Changing Quotes of

CHRIS. I. UGWOJI ESQ.

1. A leader whether at home, church, community or nation who shuns correction and positive criticism is on his way to destruction.
2. Every one's desire should be to fight to the end.
3. My prayer in my profession is that I should not allow myself to be used as an instrument of injustice whatever is the offer.
4. Injustice is deprivation of natural, human, fundamental and legal right: it is worst than Ebola disease; it should not be tolerated.
5. All that the earth or nature offers is transient, only eternity endures.
6. Success is all about determination, hard work and grace, one of which must be present but the most essential is grace.

7. If I am asked to choose three things to pass on to my children, I will choose faith in God, hard work, and peace of mind.
8. He who eats with the devil must use a long spoon but do not eat with the devil at all.
9. There is great value in personal experience.
10. Personal experience leads to great confession.
11. No one should be too big to receive and no one should be too poor to give, everyone has something to give.
12. Truth not only sets one free but brings peace of mind.
13. Peace, joy, happiness and riches are states of mind based on contentment of life and values of life.

14. Repentance is an inward transformation to an outside change of attitude and life style of a Christian.

15. Election tribunals are very important part of the electoral process. To uphold the mandate of the electorate, the tribunals should do away with all forms of legal technicality like non compliance regarding time procedure, original and non-original documents, and base their judgment on actual facts and substantial justice produced and proved before it.

16. A situation where technicality and procedure defeats the mandate of the case will not guaranty fair and free election which our tribunals are established to protect.

17. Remoteness of damage means that not every wrong doing will be sued and compensated

for. Some damages will be ignored by law as being too remote. This is also natural with human beings. Some faults will be over looked for peaceful co-existence.

18. I have always believed God of all possibilities and even when all natural, human, medical or scientific indicator points to a given conclusion, it is always important to verify with God whether that is the conclusion He desires.
19. Leadership is all about service and sacrifices to the led which is proved in action.
20. Those who left their worship centers or church because some wealthy members do not help them materially and went where they will receive material help from wealthy members are not true worshipers of God. They placed

their hope on man, rather than looking unto God.

21. I refuse to compare myself with anybody because I am not in competition with anybody rather I admire and imitate role models.

THE PROFILE OF

CHRIS. I. UGWOJI ESQ.

Chris. Iheanacho Ugwoji is a Lawyer. A graduate of University of Calabar in 1984 and Nigerian Law school in 1985, and called to Nigerian Bar on 20th August, 1985. He is in private legal practice with Victory Chambers. He is a native of Ubounkam Onicha in Ezinihitte Mbaise in Imo state of Nigeria. Born on the 4th of December 1962 to Mr. David Ugwoji whose marriage produced children of Anglican Communion. A member of Nigerian Bar Association and currently the chairman of Mbaise Branch. He loves playing or watching football.

The Life-Changing Quotes of

VEN. JOHN U. AMARAONYE

1. The only antidote against sin and evil in human life and society is the fear of God.
2. Attempt great things for God and expect great things as reward.
3. Heaven is far above as the abode of God, but God knows all we do here on earth.
4. The greatest fool on earth is somebody that says there is no God.
5. Disobedience to God and His command is as evil as sorcery and witchcraft.
6. Jesus Christ is the solid Rock of life to those that trust in Him, but a stone of judgment to those that reject Him.
7. It is not your sin that will take you to hell fire, but your rejection of Jesus Christ who will save you from sin.

8. Either you keep away from sin or sin will keep you away from Jesus Christ.
9. A life without Jesus Christ is not worth living; as such life lacks peace and hope of eternity.
10. Life has its true meaning and value when the eternal Trinity – Father, Son and the Holy Spirit is at work in it.
11. The body is the temple of the Holy Spirit; if someone provokes and sends Him out of his/her life, such person becomes a car without an engine.
12. The Bible is the greatest encyclopedia and compass of life for great visions and achievements to one that meditates on it.
13. When you refuse to take the right way of life, a compulsion to take the wrong way becomes your last option.

14. A sermon geared towards material prosperity with total neglect for salvation of souls and spiritual nourishment; is nothing but "*a gospel of stomach empowerment.*"
15. If your life is not built upon the WORD OF GOD, you are cut off from the light of life.
16. If one is not a doer of the word of God but hearer only, such person's life and endeavours are on a faulty foundation that would eventually collapse into misery and shame.
17. Profaning the law of the land is to dig a pit of destruction for yourself and your descendants.
18. As sin is a reproach to any nation, any national sin is a product of disorders, disturbances and disasters in the land.

19. Sin makes its victim a coward.
20. It is either you stand in the gap to pray out your nation or you stand together with your nation to perish.
21. Prayer is as vital as the breath of life, such that if one stops praying, he/she stops breathing spiritually.
22. The amount of time you spend to seek God is inversely proportional to God's serious attention to you.
23. Faith is believing God without questioning Him.
24. When God is with you, all your fears and terrors will become great testimonies of God's intervention.
25. Any situation that must be changed at all, must receive a divine intervention.

26. Any prayer that is not biblically based and Holy Spirit directed, is only but magical enchantment.
27. Christianity is unique and more than a religion as it is built upon the life and eternal sacrifice of Jesus Christ.
28. The cross, though rough and painful, is where all human problems have been solved.
29. The greatest mistake one would make in life is to leave this earth without making heaven.
30. Man's pride is nothing as far as he remains an obedient servant to death.
31. Righteous living makes one a general of his generation.
32. Life is a challenge of come here and make a difference

33. The greatest error in life is to live your days on earth without impacting your generation positively.
34. The great immortalization of one's name is the good legacy he/she left behind after life on earth.
35. It is not where you are that matters but what matters is what you can offer to make yourself relevant to your society.
36. The expectations on every living organism are growth and fruitfulness, a contrary to this makes one invalid as a dry wood on fire.
37. A curriculum vitae becomes unimportant when one's character passes message to the people.

38. Challenges are the spices of life which in dealing with them takes one to the next level of excellence.

39. The greatest enemy of your life is your selfish desires, which in conquering them puts all demons after life at flee.

40. Over confidence is a disease that makes somebody a popular fool.

41. A man of guilty conscience is a terror to himself, who flees when no one is pursuing him.

42. A nation that has adopted an ungodly code of law into her governance, has automatically nurtured an incurable virus disease that would send its victims to untimely death.

43. The most destructive parasite of any government is corruption; a nation free from

it would get to her greatest height of development.

44. The greatest sorrow of any generation is when an ungodly ruler is on the throne.
45. An autocratic ruler is as humble as people giving their loyalty to a terrorist.
46. Your vision gives a picture of your personality and the extent of what you can achieve in life.
47. People in agreement would build a tower from earth to heaven, as well as pull down nations with great ease.
48. A selfish leader is a misfortune to his society.
49. A man of short sightedness is a coward of great adventures.
50. When one honours God, the favour of men would come to him as a reward.

51. Marriage is divinely ordained between a man and a woman to increase and sustain life on earth, but a deviation from this Godly standard to any other form of partnership is an annihilation of human life and society.
52. The great madness on earth is when a human being partners with an animal or something else, as a man partners with his wife.
53. The happiest home is not a house with plenty of food, but a home of over flowing love among members of the family.
54. Parents contribute largely to the character of their children; reckless parents would produce reckless children, who will eventually produce a reckless society.
55. Learning has no limit, as far as a man lives, he continues to be a student to knowledge.

56. Wisdom builds a house but foolishness pulls it down with her hands.
57. Acquire wisdom and never divorce it, for in it lies your greatness and excellence.
58. Knowledge is power as commonly said, but any knowledge destined to do evil is as a human body without the head.
59. Illiteracy is a deadly disease of knowledge, which anyone infected by it is cut off from the light of civilization.
60. Every indescent dressing is a symptom of newly developing madness.

THE PROFILE OF

VEN. JOHN U. AMARAONYE

Ven. John Ugwuezi Amaraonye is an Anglican Clergyman in the Diocese of Aba (*Anglican Communion*). He was born on 11th February, 1964 at Umuihe in Isiala Ngwa South Local Government Area, of Abia state, Nigeria.

He is a theologian and educationist holding Dip.Th, B.A (*Hons*), P.G.D.E & M.Ed. He is an Ambassador of Peace and Dispute Resolution Specialist (*DRS*). He is also an intercessor, preacher, teacher and deliverance minister, and holds the office of Provincial Prayer Co-ordinator and Diocesan Prayer Co-ordinator. He as well serves as the Assistant Synod Secretary of the Diocese of Aba.

He is happily married to Mrs. Grace Ugochi Amaraonye, a health worker by profession. The marriage is blessed with four children - Chiamaka, Chukwuemeka, Chidiebube and Onyiyechi.

Presently, he serves at St. Paul's (*Ang*). Church,

Abayi Ariaria.

His hobbies are reading, writing, researching, searching the Scriptures, praying as well as singing. His utmost desire is to impact his generation positively through words of knowledge, spoken and written.

The Life-Changing Quotes of

VEN. EBENEZER E. NWOSU PhD.

1. Experience comes by years.
2. Man must honour God for man requires God to be somebody but, God does not require man to be God.
3. The yam chunk has face where it must be dipped into the palm oil before it enters the mouth.
4. 'I love you' is deep for both the man who wants a lady for a night and the one for marriage, all say I love you.
5. The stock exchange cannot lie still while the investors sleep.
6. If a would-be wife does not trust her suitor, the marriage is point-less.
7. The cooking-pot is washed for tomorrow.
8. The messenger without a message ends in mess.

9. The mad-man will only realize the need of the cane in his hand when it gets lost.
10. The anus is so good for whistling but, who would blow it is the most important thing.
11. If you are not trainable you cannot be traceable.
12. The Gospel stabilizes the Church although the Churches preach it.
13. When you are called strive to be chosen for many are called but few are chosen.
14. Leadership is taking the lead in your field.
15. Short-cut and make-up to me remains responsible for the fall in standards.
16. The problem with humanity I think is that it does not always want to remain where God wishes, but tries to stay where God does not want it be. It so dangles between miracle and

magic.

17. Leadership is not occupying position but making outstanding contributions.
18. Leadership is not teaching principles but obeying principles dedicatedly.
19. Beware of the promise or praise of humanity for if human never made you it cannot unmake you, uplift or downcast you.
20. A leader is one who knows the way, shows the way and leads the way.
21. Respect the teacher oh student for the teacher empties himself or herself into the student to make the student somebody for all things and times.
22. The Ascaris-head becomes a threat anywhere to a survivor who had once been bitten by a snake.

23. It is the ignorant that treats the snake-head as the head of an earthworm. After-all the snake head is ugly and dangerous but earthworm head is fine and friendly.
24. Vulgarity is not boldness.
25. Make-ups to some extent portray fair portraits of a blinking idiot who feels no content with nature endowment.
26. Though the ant is the most tiny animal yet, scarcely does a load dwarf it.
27. The evil from the "*Right Reverend*" does not mean right evil or right sin.
28. There could be a mad person in every community but let it not come from my family or relationship.
29. A mad one was advised to go back home, the mad retorted, 'is it all better at home'?

30. "*Let us go*" is not a man march.
31. One does not become its aim by being it but by being the best of what one is at the moment.
32. The wall that pushes down a wall does not rebuild the wall it pushed down.
33. Bad market is nothing but simply buyer-seller disagreement.
34. Give me mine is the language the market speaks.
35. Mind you, you are placed where you find yourself for others to learn from you how to do the will of God.
36. Things are in the proper direction if the world is turned Churchly but the wrong direction where the Church is turned worldly. Oh good God forbid evil.

37. If a child behaves childishly, it is lovely but should a child behave the adult way, something is wrong.

38. When the rats begin to eat wire gall, all human beings should please hide their heels.

39. The rat that bites the steel-rope alters its dentine formula.

40. Prayer is powerful without plan but more powerful should one plan and pray over a plan.

41. The best love is the stupid love for the logical love may count error logically.

42. The woman who went for war and killed a dog would kill man if she did see.

43. It is true that we learn from experiences but I would always learn from somebody else's experience.

44. The first giver is the looser.
45. The one who meets a visitor on the way, is not usually the owner of both the visitor and visit.
46. The birth of children is the cementing of a marital relationship.
47. Distortion of worship songs is not evil to a hungry person.
48. The toothpick that knows the teeth does not cause mouth-gum bleed, the one that knows them not causes mouth wound.
49. The liar annihilates a race more than world war.
50. Overdosed sinning causes long prayer says the weak prayer.
51. The powerless parent always blames own ward for causing a fight.

52. The powerless preserves the life of the war-lord.

53. Although I have no liberty to dehumanize those who propagate gender equality, but I have liberty to say that unless two things are the same, there can be no equality rather, complementing of one another.

54. Life is wealth but wealth is not life therefore wealth should be used to acquire life if possible but life should not be used to acquire wealth.

55. Anyone whose kolanut remains the last one should not present me with it to avoid telling the world about me unnecessarily.

56. The womb produces life but the tomb takes it away so they cannot agree in even sound.

57. How can the killer of a fowl say there is

plenty of meat when the killer of a cow complains of lack of meat?

58. There is equality of mortals no matter the class since all eat, excrete and exit.

59. Any comer must go no matter from which way and what time.

60. It is not wrong to eat in restaurants here if we are sure they are not found if we leave here, but carefully to know which should better prepare us for there, after here.

61. May we be committed enough not to remember God only in times of trouble also in times of pleasure.

62. How can there be priesthood of all believers or is it rather all believers emulating the believing priesthood?

63. Speak well in the presence of the Lord or

rather keep quiet in mouth and mind.

64. Modern penitents dress well to church and dress anyhow on the streets but my worry is, ‘are the two not public’? If public then public dressing has been and should be descent dressing to avoid decent misunderstanding and misinterpretation.

THE PROFILE OF

VENERABLE EBENEZER E. NWOSU

Venerable, Ebenezer E. Nwosu, is a missionary in the Anglican Communion. He was ordained in 1994. Since his call to Holy Order, he has headed many congregations, parishes and archdeaconries. He has also held many administrative positions including: Pioneer Clerical Synod Secretary of Diocese of Isiala Ngwa South, Bishop's Administrative Assistant and Diocesan Overseas Relations Officer, Diocese of Aba Ngwa North, etc.

Academically, he has nearly been schooling and is not tired of learning. He has: Diploma in Theology (*Dip Theo. Trinicol.*), Dip RS Unical., B.A Ed. 2nd Class Upper, UNN, M.A and PhD in Religion, Uniport, Nigeria. He also had Alternative Dispute Resolution Training in 2012 qualifying him as Dispute Resolution Specialist (*DRS*). He loves teaching and has lectured since 2008.

He is married to Mrs. G. Ugodia Nwosu, B.Ed. a teacher by profession and the marriage is blessed with three children, Onyeuwaoma, Amarachi and Chioma. Although a native of Itungwa, Obingwa LGA Abia State, he was born in Port Harcourt where his Christian parents, Mr James Dinna and Mrs Regina Ezimma Nwosu, the two are of blessed memory, were living at that time. Venerable Nwosu has as hobby, footballing, singing, reading and writing and entertaining friends. Loves order, straight-forwardness and is jovial and kind. He is a Christian.

E. Enyioma Nwosu, PhD,DRS.
(31-8-2015)

The Life-Changing Quotes of

VEN. GOKA MUELE MPIGI. PhD

1. A child that is tied to his mother's back does not know how far the journey is.
2. It takes time to dissect the ant to know what is inside its stomach.
3. The luck star does not appear in the sky every night.
4. If hunters have learnt how to shoot without missing; birds will also learn how to fly without perching.
5. He who brings home ant-infested firewood should not complain when lizards come visiting.
6. A child who does not allow his mother to sleep shall equally not sleep.
7. No matter how old a lion is, it will never eat grass.
8. He who buys happiness with his tears smiles

forever.

9. Great leaders are products of good followership.
10. Whatever you take for granted today will ask you a question tomorrow.
11. Leadership deprives one of right to mercy.
12. A good leader should be in control and not in charge.
13. Divide and rule destroys but unite and rule builds.
14. What an elder sees while sitting cannot be seen by the young man on the tree.
15. Integrity adds value to one's life.
16. A friend is one who has the same enemies as I have.
17. For a man to succeed, he must be at the right place at the right time.

18. If you don't like me, you must get to know me better.

19. No matter how slow I walk, you will never come to meet me at the same spot.

20. If you insist on knowing what the content of happiness is, you will never be happy.

21. The plantain tree that obeys the wind can never be pulled down by the wind.

22. At the heart of all beauty lies something inhuman.

23. A bended heart cannot be broken.

24. If you choose to be different, then expect to be lonely.

THE PROFILE OF
VEN. GOKA MUELE MPIGI. PhD.

VEN. GOKA MUELE MPIGI. ***PhD*** is an Archdeacon of Church of Nigeria, Anglican Communion. Born on 14th, February 1974, Goka is a native of Koroma in Tai Local Government Area of Rivers State, Nigeria. He is married with Children. He is a Lecturer at Rev D. O. Ockiya College of Science And Theology, Ogbia, Bayelsa State; and Akwa Ibom State University. He holds Diploma in Theology (*1994*), Trinity Theological College Umuahia, Nigeria; Bachelor of Arts (*BA*) Religion (*2000*), University Of Nigeria, Nsukka; Master of Arts (*MA*) Religious and Cultural Studies (*2007*), University Of Port Harcourt, Nigeria; Master of Theology (*M.Th*) Systematic Theology (2012), Crowther Graduate Theological Seminary, Abeokuta, Nigeria; Doctor of Philosophy (*PhD*) 2014, University of Port Harcourt, Nigeria.

The Life-Changing Quotes of

HART O. HART

1. One word for all of God's Laws and Commandments is LOVE and the worst sin is its opposite HATRED.
2. If you are moving in the right direction don't stop moving for you will arrive at the right place.
3. Sustain your world through the Word of God for God's words have all dream seeds for the sustenance of your world.
4. Love is the key to all good things of life. Love is wisdom and Love is life so get love and quickly forgive.
5. Life without the right divine worship is vague, meaningless and purposeless.
6. Don't cheat to succeed for the measure you give you must get.

7. There is very great wisdom in keeping quiet especially when you are not sure of what you are saying. For fools talk when it is not necessary.

8. If you have Christ you have love therefore relax for you have the clue to all the wonders of love and life.

9. Admire your dreams; don't just be pressured down by circumstances to forsake them rather nurture and build them with bricks if you want to live and not just to exist.

10. The world is existing and is sustained by co-creators with God who cannot let go of their dreams until it becomes reality.

11. You have finally fallen when you finally refuse to rise.

12. We must aspire so much to be the revival we want to revive.

13. If you are not satisfied or happy with your now and you want to change your tomorrow then alter your today's decision by changing to positive thoughts, for the consequences of your tomorrow are the actions of your today.

14. Don't plan to save when you have millions, learn to live according to your earnings today and no matter how small just try and be able to save for future.

15. Being Christ-like or one in Christ is when you have become someone for others and that is worship/service to God.

16. Remold your now with good and positive thought, actions and determination to enjoy your tomorrow.

17. If you avoid or refuse to accept your God given assignment, God may let painful experience to permit correction.

18. Forgiveness paves way to concordant relationship with your neighbor and your creator.

19. No matter where ever you are divinely placed provision is always there.

20. Your background can never keep your back to the ground if you don't want to.

21. A lead is like the pipe through which the oil or the living water from God flows to God's children. He must keep himself pure

and clean to avoid giving out rusted or toxic water.

22. Walking in love is the evidence of the Christ-likeness in us and the reason why we are called Christians and the evidence that we are God's Children.

23. Don't just only read the Bible but live the Bible to quit existing and start living.

24. Just dare for a worthy cause and don't be afraid of failure for it is even better to try and fail than to be at the mediocre place where you can neither achieve success nor defeat.

25. Your thoughts mold your destiny. What you mostly think is what you're bound to be. To remold your destiny think and act positively and you will change your world.

26. No matter how bright the sun is it will fade. No matter how beautiful the flowers it will wither one day. Nothing is permanent. For the ugly old people you see now were the beautiful ones of yester years, so respect and honour the aged.

27. Indolence produces obscurity but diligence produces success.

28. Man is better weighed on the balance of choices he makes or takes during challenging and conflicting moments and not in periods of comfort.

29. Happiness and sadness is a matter of choice not circumstances

30. Why say that the sky is the limit when men have walked in the moon.

31. Gratitude is a great virtue that is only for the wise.

32. Before you can get testimony(s), you must see your helplessness and the need to pray until something happens.

33. A genuine altar for prayer will change your destiny and eliminate your limitations.

34. Better desire a befitting life than a befitting burial for the later is much better. The worth of you is not what you name yourself after but the worth of your impact in the world.

35. Access to revelational knowledge is the key secret to everlasting wealth.

36. The access to God's presence is the greatest ascent of man.

37. If you don't work you cannot worth.

38. Faithlessness stops miracles.

39. It is natural to be envied when you succeed for people don't envy failures.

40 Friendship is a choice not birth.

41. Love is a choice.

42. Recreate your life for life is a gift from God and therefore has value.

43. Rediscover how unique you are for nothing is as beautiful as realizing your uniqueness.

44. You can possibly increase your values by just being in love with your life and yourself.

45. A woman's beauty may attract a relationship (husband) but it is her character that will sustain it.

46. Your nature forms your character or who you are when no one is looking and your character determines your future.

47. Pain is part of life and a fact but suffering is optional.

48. Why do we say that the sky is the limit when there are footprints above the sky?

49. Happiness and sadness is a matter of choice not circumstances.

50. Gratitude is the virtue of only the wise.

51. The worth of a man is not weighed when he stands in comfort but on the choices he makes or takes during conflicting and challenging moments.

THE PROFILE OF
Hart O. Hart

Hart O. Hart was one of the musicians in Revd. Canon Okolo's music group in Jos who also sponsored Hart's debut gospel music called "This Time", recorded at Panam Music world. He later became an Anglican Pastor in the year 2000, after his Bachelor's Degree in Divinity at Theological College in Northern Nigeria, Bukuru. He and the wife Chibiko and children Praise-God and Chimaranma are presently with the Diocese of Aba Ngwa North, Abia State, Nigeria.

The Life-Changing Quotes of

VEN. OKIKE OSISIOGU

1. Preaching is not all about rhetoric oratory or motivational or high sounding words but a reflection of the life of Christ in the everyday life of the preacher.
2. The flesh loves to give correction but does not take correction, loves to lead but does not want to be led, desires to give instruction but does not take instruction.
3. God is not an aloof God who sits in heaven watching and seeing mortal man destroy and desecrate the things He has carefully created.
4. The goal of Christian leadership and discipleship is not to make one Christian to be like another Christian but to conform to the image and likeness of Christ.

5. Before your message conquers your congregation or audience, it will first and foremost conquer you.
6. Come let us reason together is an expression of the humility of the God we worship in Christ, in the same vein; we should be humble in our dealing with one another irrespective of our position and attainment.
7. The phrase son of man used several times in the book of Ezekiel is a reminder to mortal man that he is first and foremost the son of man before any and every other attainment in life - Doctor, Lawyer, Accountant, Teacher, Business Mogul, Pharmacist, Engineer etc.
8. Spiritual warfare is 24 hour war/battle that goes on in the spirit world against Satan and his agents.

9. Revival is not dancing while the gospel band is being played but a renewed obedience to obey the Word of God and willingness to repent and forsake the life of sin.
10. One of the ways we need to win in our battle against the devil and the forces of darkness is the area of inferiority complex. Israel suffered complex because of the threats of Goliath the Philistine giant until David came on board and the story changed for good for Israel.
11. Pentecost has ceased to be ordinary Jewish festival to a time of the outpouring of the Holy Spirit and God's visitation upon His people. May you experience it based on the later definition.
12. The Holy Spirit is that spirit that moved on the face of the water when the earth was

without form and void and contributed immensely in giving the earth shape and form.(*Gen.1:2*)

13. Jesus is the bread of life, also implies that He feeds His people both spiritually and with the physical food. His feeding of the 5,000 and 4,000 respectively is a case in point.
14. Meekness is the life of somebody that is defending nothing but allows the Will of God to be made manifest in his or her life.
15. True prosperity is not all about utility Gospel but absolute trust and reliance that God is able to provide the daily food and need of His people.
16. Repentance is not about ordinary church membership but a two way u-turn viz:

turning away from the life of sin and turning towards the direction of God.

17. God was in Christ reconciling the world unto Himself and now has given His mandate to His people to partner with Him to reconcile their fellow human beings to Himself.
18. The Great Commission is all about disciplining men for Christ and making them useable instrument in His hands.
19. Let this mind that was in Christ Jesus also be in you. The elder brother of the prodigal son did not have his father's type of mind hence his anger on the return of his lost only brother.
20. Let the children first be fed is an expression that God's children are number one in his

agenda. Are you one of His children? Expect to be first fed by Him.

21. For you to become anything tangible in the sight of God, your faith ought to be tried like gold and you came out refined.

22. Elisha went with his master Elijah to Bethel, Jericho and Jordan all in the deliberate search of a double portion of his master's spirit. For you to get the fullness of God's power you must be willing to pay the price of going with our Master Jesus to any location of His leading upon your life. (*2 Kings 2:1-9*).

23. You may be that man that God Almighty sought for to stand in the gap and make up the hedge but did not find (*Ezek. 22:30*) as you give your life to Christ and dedicate your life for His service.

24. Everywhere He went He was doing good, healing all manner of diseases and casting out devils. He cannot stop being and doing good with our generation. All we need to do is to trust Him in every situation of life.
25. You cannot overcome an enemy except you first and foremost overcome his strongholds.
26. One of the reasons why God established His church is to speak against evil.
27. God has a thousand and many ways of doing His things and speaking to His people.
28. Our small life is too small to be managed by the God who manages the earth and heaven.
29. You shall seek Me and find Me when you seek Me with all your heart not your head or your philosophical ideas.

30. In the Lord's Prayer, we pray for a kingdom but in the church of today we have settled for mere power and power tussle.

31. The wagon sent by Joseph to convey his earthly father Jacob to the land of Egypt revived the spirit of his father Jacob. Praise and worship is a vehicle that revives and gladdens the heart of our heavenly father no wonder the Scripture says that God inhabits on the praises of His people. Give it to Him in full dosage.

32. David killed Goliath the Philistine giant with five smooth stones that represents the name of Jesus. Indeed the Name of the Lord is a strong tower, the righteous runs into it and is safe. Have you run to Him for safety and deliverance?

33. If you make a mistake in the foundation of a building it will affect the entire structure. The mistake of foundation hurts one all through his life, except by God's intervention.
34. One of the problems, wonderings and lack of focus and direction we have in life is as a result of improper foundation.
35. Invite Jesus into your marriage, you will never regret it or be embarrassed. The wedding of Cana of Galilee is a case in point.
36. Prosperity is one of the contents of the Gospel but not the whole Gospel. Preach the full Gospel.
37. God did not create us to occupy space or to fulfill all the righteousness of creation but to use us to affect our generation for Him

through a consistent life of absolute surrender and yieldedness.

38. Take this child and nurse him for me is not just the word of Pharaoh's daughter to the mother of Moses but God's mandate to His church to involve in aggressive evangelism and Christian discipleship to children of all ages.

39. You are a reflection of the person that disciples you. A disciple is not greater than his master.

40. The sickness that took the devil 38 years to plant in a man's life took Jesus a sentence to correct viz Rise, take up thy bed and walk.

41. Good work alone cannot guarantee salvation but absolute surrender of one's life to Jesus.

42. If you are willing and obedient you will eat the fruit of the land. The land in question means your country; your state, your town; your business or profession etc.

43. Your life should teach the world the righteousness; holiness of God and the correct way of life.

44. Integrity is all about being upright, faithful, transparent and straightforward. Indeed integrity is what you do.

45. An ounce of obedience is worth more than a ton of prayer.

46. Your choices of yesterday are a determinant factor of your position today.

47. Giving is part of the worship we render to God and not necessarily to carry out one

project or the other, though it could be used for God's project.

48. Yes God is not the God of abandoned project if He is duly carried along and consulted at the inception of the project.

49. My son give me your heart suggests that God is more interested in getting our heart saved before any other thing.

50. The challenges facing our generation suggests that we should paraphrase the hymn, *I need thee every hour* to *I need thee every second*, one hour is too far away not to be with our God.

51. The price that good/Godly men pay for not speaking out and keeping quiet is to be ruled by evil men.

52. As Paul left the young minister Titus in Crete to put things in order, so has God left and

placed you where you are now to put things in order. As a Christian, you are supposed to insist that things are done the right way when you are around.

53. The grace of God that bringeth salvation has appeared to all men (*Titus 2:11*). All men here implies the white, black, the rich, the poor, the educated, non-educated etc. Don't exempt yourself from the salvation that the grace of God brought to mankind.
54. In the world you will have tribulation (*John 16:33*) suggests that there is no problem free world. All you need to do is to be cheerful about and look unto God for solutions to your problem.

55. The Tabernacle of the righteous is the supposed place for rejoicing and praise worship.

56. It is amazing to note that He was oppressed and afflicted, yet He did not open His mouth in defense of Himself. Don't be anxious to defend yourself. God will rise in your defense.

57. God is very passionate about His love for people hence the statement, *for Zion's sake I will not hold my peace and for Jerusalem's sake I will not rest.* How do you reciprocate to this in your worship and devotion to this gesture of the love of God?

58. Your prayer for your enemies should not be for them to fall and die but *"Father forgive them for they know not what they do".*

59. The Monster, Anger deprived Moses the privileged from taking the Israelites to the Promised Land. Decisively deal with this monster in your own life.

60. To die is gain only applies to those who died in the Lord. Prepare to live for the Lord and die in Him.

61. Knowledge is the acquiring of facts; understanding is the interpretation of facts, while wisdom is the right application of facts.

62. You are not in the world necessarily to catch up with your mates but to live and serve out the purpose of God in your life.

PROFILE OF
VEN. OKIKE OSISIOGU

Ven. Okike Osisiogu was born at Enugu to Mr. Jeremaiah Nwabueze and Mrs. Remi Ihunanya Osisiogu (*both of blessed memory*) of Umuobutu Village, Old Umuahia Autonomous Community in Umuahia South Local Government Area of Abia State.

Okike had his Primary School at Udi Road Primary School (*formerly St. Bartholomew's Primary School*), Asata, Enugu after which he went through two Secondary Schools viz: Government College Umuahia and Boys Secondary School Awhum and finished in the year 1983.

After his Secondary School, he worked in the following establishments: Jot Lims Laundry Nigeria Limited, Selins Jugo Nigeria Ltd., and Victory Christian Firm. In 1991, in response to the call of God upon his life, he joined the ministry in the Diocese of Aba as a Church Teacher. He was selected by Rt. Rev. Prof. Augustine O. Iwuagwu (*then Bishop of Aba*) for ministerial training at St. Paul's College Awka (*now Paul's University*) and in 1995 he completed with Diploma Theology, Awka, and Diploma Religious Studies, University of Nigeria Nsukka. He was made a Deacon on 2nd July 1995 and Priested on 7th July 1996 all by the Rt. Rev. Prof. Augustine O. Iwuagwu. He was preferred a CANON in Sept. 2002 by Rt. Rev. Augustine Iwuagwu (*Rtd.*) and an Archdeacon in 2006 by Most Rev. Ugochukwu Uwaoma Ezuoke (*Rtd.*). In pursuance of further studies, Okike went through the then Rivers State College of Education Port-Harcourt in Affiliation with University of Ibadan and passed out successfully with 2nd Class honours of the University of Ibadan.

God has used him with others to plant many Churches as well as carry out missionary outreaches in many areas. Prior to his call into the ministry, Okike held positions in many Christian organizations which includes: the Evangelical Fellowship in the Anglican

Communion (*EFAC*), Scripture Union (*SU*), Anglican Youth Fellowship (*AYF*), etc.

Ven. Okike is happily married to Mrs. Florence Osisiogu, a Laboratory Scientist and Lecturer, Department of Microbiology, Abia State Polytechnic, Aba and the union is blessed with a son and four daughters.

His hobbies include among others, mission/soul winning, traveling, listening to music, working for the unity of the body of Christ.

The Life-Changing Quotes of

BRO. EBERE NWANKWO

1. A discipled businessman understands that the principle of growth is in savings and re-investing and not in wasting.
2. When a youth saves three active hours of his youthful age for siesta, he will harvest more than five hours of his old age to keep awake.
3. When you refuse to work hard when your age mates are working, you will labour when your age mates are enjoying.
4. You set the clock in your house but God sets the time and seasons for everything.
5. When you refuse to work on the road of hard work, honesty and truth, you operate on the highway of poverty and lack.
6. The skill exhibited by David was acquired in the bush with the sheep not in the palace.

7. To David faith is, put all your weapons in God, watch and let God fight the battle.
8. David understood that the Name of God was greater than any Goliath and his armour put together.
9. David learnt the principle of self development while shepherding the flock.
10. David learnt the act of healthy living while feeding on the table of God's green pastures.
11. Your reaction in time of challenges or troubles speak volume.
12. Your performance on your duty post gives the voice of professionalism or unskilled.
13. Everything God created has voice without verbalizing it.
14. Your emotions, intelligence, professionalism and hard work build a mansion for money.

15. When you build a house for money in Christ with honesty as the major building material it serves your blood line.
16. Creativity is in the conscious and sub-conscious while authorship will be manifested with the hands.
17. When you think with your heart, brain and stomach you will maintain good relationships and healthy living.
18. As you think with your God-given brain cells, you must realize that God did not give others saw-dusts, if you do you will have a shipwreck in your relationship.
19. Creativity and authorship comes from the womb of the mind.

20. The greatest womb given to human beings is the womb of the mind, high-rise buildings, cars, money making were all conceived there.
21. When you are not trained most of your visions will die in the womb of the mind.
22. For healthy living, wealth creation, relationship, eat balanced diets for your body, the Word of God for your spirit, good thoughts, Psalms, songs of praise for your soul.
23. There are classes of marriage, those managing to live under one roof and those living as stipulated and enjoying in pains or joy.
24. A road that is cleaned on one side is the same as a sick marriage but when it is cleared on

both sides it is the same as a healthy marriage.

25. The worst sickness is that of mindset. David prevailed against Goliath when the trained solders hid themselves for forty days.
26. When you don't invest healthy spiritual values in your children, you will end up raising a straying bloodline.
27. The best investment in your child is the Word of God, prayers, hardwork, honest etc you will have a voice in your family tie.
28. The joy in spirit (*alcohol*) is cosmetic but that of the Holy Spirit is real and lasting with good health.
29. When you have the Holy Spirit as your Teacher, He will give you God's blueprints when He created everything He created.

30. God does not teach a folded hand and mind how to create wealth.
31. Any leadership without a success is a failure.
32. A servant leader uses his stomach and head to watch and preserve those he leads while a strong natural leader cares for no one and for no one else.
33. Esau having sold his birth right for one course meal took a tag that disqualified him as a leader who preserves but one who will even sell his subjects for one course meal as well.
34. A good leader is like a conduct pipe that has many outlets reaching the rich, the poor and the lowly.
35. Abraham and Lot were leaders, the legacy Abraham left for us speaks of blessing while Lot left no posterity.

36. A good leader will avoid words that inflate pride and wound charity.
37. A valiant soldier with a good armour bearer is in the same shoes with an executive governor with good cabinet members, they will always deliver good governance for their subjects.
38. A valiant soldier with a good armour will shoot with both hands without missing his targets.
39. A good leader's legacy is his military power to crush his enemies and protect his subjects.
40. A good leader's legacy is his religious power to direct their spirits (*his subjects*).
41. A good leader's legacy is his intellectual power to direct both soul and mind.

42. A good leader builds on the strong points of his people not on their weak points.
43. When you abstain from physical training you will not have self development.
44. Mental development is the catalyst for self development.
45. It is better to be a thermostat who dictates the temperature of the environment than a thermometer that adapts to the temperature of the environment.
46. If you don't cage the tongue as a leader, you will dig the grave of your throne.
47. When the leader with a spiritual cataract and glaucoma does not have a spiritual eye doctor in his cabinet, both the throne and the subjects will operate on the highways and bye-ways designed for the blind.

THE PROFILE OF

BRO. EBERE ANUBA GABRIEL NWANKWO

Bro Ebere Anuba Gabriel Nwankwo is from Uratta in Isiala Ngwa North L.G.A. had his primary school at Uratta Community School, Secondary at Eziama High School Aba and had a Certificate curse in Bubaling.

Learned lay minister of Anglican Church, has been in deliverance ministry and member intercession for Nigeria.

Married with two boys and a girl.

The Life-Changing Quotes of

MRS. CHINURU UZOIJE

1. Shyness results to inferiority complex and keeps one withdrawn, but boldness and courage places one over and above his/her equals.
2. Come out of yourself and the stuff you are made of, will be revealed.
3. Leadership is not learned, it's inspired.
4. The earth has no sorrow which the heaven cannot bear.
5. Stand up to your feet and say no to your defeat.
6. Talk less of what is working against you and talk more of what is working for you.
7. Little minds gossip but matured minds discuss issues.
8. Whatsoever you vividly imagine and honestly desire must inevitably come to pass.

9. Your speech creates your future, be reminded that there's power in spoken words.
10. Cordial relationship between parents and children leads to transparency and openness from the children.
11. One minute interaction with a child will destroy thousand and one negative thoughts in his/her mind/heart.
12. Dialogue is the best way to calm tension in marriage. Endeavour to bridge that communication gap.
13. It takes two to make a bed, if a husband and wife are not in agreement they can't make any head way in their relationship.
14. Submission attracts love, when a woman submits, the husband shows love.

15. Marriage is meant to be enjoyed and not endured.

16. Sensitivity in the spirit helps one to identify his/her unfriendly friend at home, at your workplace and in marriage.

17. Bad attitude is like a broken rotten egg that smells continuously until it is thrown away. Unless you do away with it, people will keep isolating you. Ask God to help you change them or else you will remain like stagnant water.

18. Man is powerless, hopeless when his dependence is not on God.

19. Encounter with God is meant for transformation of life. You must hold God tenaciously, never let Him go, until

something remarkable happens. Encounter Him and get all the benefits.

20. When one fails to appreciate God for all He has done in his/her life, he/she will begin to depreciate.
21. A minute chance given to the devil can cause a million damages.
22. Logical thinking and intuition are keys to creativity.
23. Logical thinkers are great achievers.
24. Sit down and analyse situations before you take decision.
25. Never stop preparing for your future because there is no limit to your potentials.
26. Once you believe in yourself, you can make a difference in the world.

27. The choice you make has consequences, it can make or mar you.
28. A little side attraction from your guess on God, can rub you eternity and the race will be in vain.
29. Create room in your heart to desire and study the Word of God in order to be active in Him.
30. When we bow our knees to God, our needs will bow before us.
31. Conflict management and resolution calms organizational crisis, apply it.
32. Conducive working environment creates room for efficient performance.
33. A small skill acquired today, with little capital, high concentration and zeal can burst into a large conglomerate tomorrow.

34. Hard work is the basic tool to achieving your desired career/ambition.
35. The brain as an engine room harbours diverse thoughts, make the right choice inorder to succeed.
36. Life of pretence is a gateway to falsehood, make a u-turn.
37. Decisions based on emotions can be destructive.
38. Stay positive, calm and exhibit humility always.
39. Aligning yourself with the right company places you on a better pedestrian/footing.
40. Nagging is always resentful and is a bad way to communicate.

41. Being around good people can develop your character and intellect. Never resist wise counsel.

THE PROFILE OF CHINURU UZOIJE (*MRS.*)

Chinuru G. Uzoije is an Anglican in both Aba and Aba Ngwa North Diocese. She was born into a Christian family in Amaogwugwu in Umuahia North Local Government Area of Abia State, Nigeria.

She attended Santa Maria, now Constitution Crescent Primary School and Immaculate Heart, now Community Girls' Secondary School Umungasi Aba, Abia State, respectively.

She had a B.Sc in Banking and Finance from Abia State University Uturu, Post Graduate Diploma in Education in University of Calabar and a Masters Degree in Accountancy from Michael Okpara University of Agriculture Umudike. She is currently a teacher in the Secondary Education Management Board, Umuahia. She is committed to God's work. Chinuru Uzoije's marriage to Mr. Bethel

Okechukwu J. Uzoije of Amavo Village in Ugwunagbo Local Government Area of Abia State is blessed with four (*4*) lovely and God fearing children.

The Life-Changing Quotes of

MR. ERNEST UZOMA NWANKPA

1. Who is a rich man? The man whose children run into his arms whenever his hands are empty.
2. Never judge each day by the harvest you reap, but by the seeds that you plant.
3. Perfection may not be easily achieved but if we chase perfection, we can catch excellence.
4. The horses in front determine the pace of horses at the back.
5. A virtuous woman converts a recalcitrant husband, floats a spirit-filled church and builds a peaceful society.
6. What you give to the mirror equals what you receive from it.
7. If you absent from truth, you remain absent.
8. A man that terms himself clever ends up committing major blunders.

9. Obstacles are those things that come our way when we lose sight of our goal.
10. Love is obeying God's injunctions and obeying God's injunctions is hating sin.
11. A consensus is collective agreement which no one believes individually.
12. Sanity is checkmating madness in order to make good use of it.
13. Be wise in making proverbs not as a fool who repeats it.
14. Positive thinking is expecting the best to happen at its right time.
15. Creativity is in-exhaustive, the more you crave, the more you create.
16. Think everything but don't believe everything.

17. The strongest weapon to fight over darkest moment is to extract the light inherent in it.
18. If you recognize your madness, you have sanity.
19. Education is a gateway to chase out our ignorance.
20. Sleep is better enjoyed when dead.
21. Refinement of everyday thinking is nothing but the whole of science.
22. Education is a repository of all forgotten learning while in school.
23. Ideas have no wings but they fly.
24. Culture does not speak but identifies.
25. Perfection is not perfect when there is no more to take away.
26. Knowledge builds, wisdom decorates.

27. When one door of happiness closes, another opens but due to our concentration on the closed door, we lose sight of the opened one.
28. It is better to go for the best than better because the best needs no addition.
29. You are your thought and your thought is you outside.
30. Woman is a person wooed by man to be his wo-man.
31. Your attitude to life determines your altitude in life.
32. Lifting someone up is a step to lifting yourself up.
33. He who stays in bed, thinking he will make money staying in bed, will lack sleep.
34. Success is valueless if its value is not attached.

35. If you seize an opportunity, you create manipulation.
36. Be careful in life because what you said and what you did can be forgotten but not how you made people feel.
37. Fear knocks on a door and faith went to open but found nobody.
38. Learn to forgive your enemies but don't forget their names.
39. Someone cannot help everyone but everyone can help someone.
40. If you avoid reality, be ready to face the consequences of reality.
41. Don't play down on anything that sets your soul on fire.
42. Everything is standstill, until you make it to move.

43. If you have never made a mistake, you have never tried anything new.
44. Achieving peace is a matter of understanding.
45. The world is what it is because man has refused to make it what it ought to be.
46. What makes a man what he is? That is what he is.
47. Corruption is what it is today because corrupt people have refused to be corrected.
48. When your face becomes oblong, you dwarf your lifespan.
49. As our eyes catch certain things, it is important we pursue only those that capture the heart.
50. Your destiny is destined to become the person you decide to be.

51. Nothing is impossible because impossible declares I'm possible.
52. He who goes about gossiping against others is building up structures that will imprison him.
53. If you say there is no God, try looking for a mechanic on Sunday.
54. A man at the age of 35 who lacks liberality has no heart; a man at the age of 40 who lacks conservations, has no brains.
55. The decision to act is the beginning of business.
56. If you fail to build your dreams, others will hire you to build theirs.
57. If you hear any voice that says "*you can't*", blot out "*t*" and then you can.
58. An extravagant person eats into his future.

59. Finance is the engine that propels business but driven by human brain.

THE PROFILE OF

MR. ERNEST UZOMA NWANKPA

Mr. Ernest Uzoma Nwankpa was born some fifty nine years ago to the family of Late Mr. & Mrs. Ezekiel Chino and Josephine N. Nwankpa in Okpu Umuobo Autonomous Community in Osisioma Ngwa Local Government Area of Abia State, Nigeria.

He had his Primary Six in 1973 and Secondary School in 1978. He had gone through various academic trainings. He holds B.Sc Degree in Accountancy.

He has worked in various private establishments and presently the Central Office Administrator in the Diocese of Aba Ngwa North of Church of Nigeria, Anglican Communion.

He is happily married to Mrs. Roseline Nwaezinma Uzoma with three children: Daberechukwu, Amarachukwu and Chinemerem.

The Life-Changing Quotes of

LADY SALLY NNE UNAM (DM)

1. Regard challenges as opportunities for growth and achieve success inspite of them by developing trust in God.
2. As a leader, delegate responsibilities properly.
3. Supervise, only by so doing will you ensure that the job delegated is done.
4. Be diligent and honest, God rewards hard work.
5. Resist the temptation to give your body in exchange for "*dirty*" money.
6. Do not use your position to interfere with funds. Let the appropriate officer be in charge, that way you ensure proper accountability.
7. Always be prepared to serve both God and man.

8. Don't just be honest; let it be obvious that you are.
9. Never loose moral values.
10. Determine to make a success of your marriage by being faithful, tolerant, patient and loving. Giving to every family member what they require even when it hurts.
11. Have confidence in every member of your family, treating everyone equally.
12. Different environments pose different challenges therefore, never feel inferior to anyone black or white.
13. Remain focused inspite of jealousies and antagonisms.
14. Ignore accusations. Be sincere and remain steadfast. The truth must vindicate you.

15. If you suspect diabolic acts against you, and they exist, do not ignore them, counter them with the Word of God and with prayers.
16. Be prayerful always. Our society is ridden with evil.
17. Trust God to see you through and He will.
18. Do not expect the whole world to jubilate over your successes.
19. Bear no grudge against anyone.
20. Be loving and forgiving that you may have peace.
21. Fear God, serve man.
22. Take responsibility for your decisions and actions.
23. Cultivate friendships, you never know tomorrow.

24. Keep healthy by undertaking regular physical exercises.
25. Read, to widen your knowledge.
26. Travel is educating. It does wonders to your confidence.
27. Aim to excel.
28. Don't stagnate. Get up and go.
29. Persevere; the all knowing God knows your problem.
30. Always be a moderating influence.
31. For manifestation of your dreams, have vision, be desirous, accept that it is possible, believe it shall be achieved, be sure your intentions are genuine, take action, let go and let God do the rest.
32. Have an itinerary for your daily tasks.

33. Prioritize and carry over tasks in order of priority.
34. It is wise to make notes of important dates and events both past, present and future.
35. Diary keeping on a daily basis helps you to remember things.
36. Like the Bible is indispensable, use it to improve your vocabulary.
37. Don't be like the Joneses. Be yourself.
38. A goal without a plan is just a wish.
39. Insist on principles in raising your children.
40. Respect should start from the home.
41. Personal hygiene is a must.
42. If you don't value your time, neither will others.
43. If you don't value yourself, neither will others value you.

44. No problem can be solved from the same level of consciousness that created it.
45. Concentration proceeds understanding which begets knowledge leading to success.
46. Looking is not seeing. Make sure to see.
47. Euthusiasm removes obstacles.
48. Courage is the greatest of all virtues because from it all other qualities proceed.
49. Make yourself a force to reckon with by exhibiting high moral standards.
50. Endeavour to strike the balance between family, work, church and community.
51. The greatest gift a father can give to his children is himself.
52. Seek God's wisdom in all things.
53. The storms of our life prove the strength of our anchor.

54. Never waste your time trying to explain who you are to people who are committed to misunderstanding you.
55. Have more than you show, and speak less than you know.
56. Truth is vital. Speak it.
57. Live without trying to convince the world that you have life.
58. Worry about your character and not your reputation because your character is who you are and your reputation is only what people think of you.
59. If material things are what you are talking about when you say "*I am blessed*," you have no idea about blessing.
60. In the home, if everything has a place, order is established and time is saved.

BRIEF BIOGRAPHY OF EZINNE, DAUGHTER OF ZION, UNIQUE MOTHER, ROLE MODEL

LADY SALLY NNE UNAM (*DM*)

Born of Royalty. Attended Primary and Secondary Schools in Port-Harcourt in River State. Obtained HND in Business Studies (*WITH DISTINCTION*) in London in 1967 winning the WARREN PRIZE as Best Student.

Hold a Post Graduate Diploma in Personnel Administration, and the Basic Health and Safety Certificate of Chartered Institute of Environment Health (*UK*).

Attended many Courses

Having years working experience in both gainful and self-employment. A Past Board Director of International Inner wheel, I have held various Leadership positions and received many Awards of Merit.

Married with five children and eleven grandchildren.

ABOUT THE AUTHOR

Sam Nnodim is a Professional in the field of Information Technology (IT). He is proficient in publishing; having raised many published authors and published several titles.

He is the Managing Director/CEO of SAMDIM COMPUTERS AND BUSINESS SERVICES; a computer firm, which has over the years excelled by providing reliable and time tested solutions to individual and business needs using modern technology.

ABOUT THE BOOK

The wealth of wisdom is a collection of life experiences and observations of distinguished leaders and notable achievers.

Sam Nnodim collected the wisdom of these elders in order to ensure that lessons learned from our elders are preserved and passed on to the younger generation.

These great elders are people of honour and loyalty whose labour have shaped our loyalty. The women and men included in this life-changing masterpiece represents the excellence of our ambience.

These great elders are Chris. Iheanacho Ugwoji, Ven. John Ugwuezi Amaraonye, Venerable Ebenezer E. Nwosu, Ven. Goka Muele Mpigi, PhD, Hart O. Hart, Ven. Okike Osisiogu, Bro Ebere Anuba Gabriel Nwankwo, Mrs. Chinuru G. Uzoije, Mr. Ernest Uzoma Nwankpa and Lady Sally Nne Unam (*DM*). They are the writers of this masterpiece.

This masterpiece will empower everyone who is ready to leave a legacy to build the strength, courage and wisdom needed to make a distinctive difference.

www.ingramcontent.com/pod-product-compliance
Lightning Source LLC
LaVergne TN
LVHW041159080426
835511LV00006B/663
* 9 7 8 9 7 8 5 0 3 3 7 7 9 *